Th

D0052137

To

_____

From

_____

Date

_____

Message

_____

_____

My
LITTLE
BOOK OF
prayers

christian
art gifts

My Little Book of Prayers

© 2002 Christian Art Gifts, PO Box 1599, Vereeniging, 1930, South Africa

Compiled by Lynette Douglas
Designed by Christian Art Gifts

Christian Art Gifts has made every effort to trace the ownership of all quotes and poems in this book. In the event of any question that may arise from the use of any quote or poem, we regret any error made and will be pleased to make the necessary correction in future editions of this book.

Unless otherwise indicated, Scripture taken from the HOLY BIBLE, NEW INTERNATIONAL VERSION. Copyright 1973, 1978, 1984 International Bible Society. Used by permission of Zondervan Bible Publishers.

ISBN 1-86920-061-6

Printed in Hong Kong

02 03 04 05 06 07 08 09 10 11 – 10 9 8 7 6 5 4 3 2 1

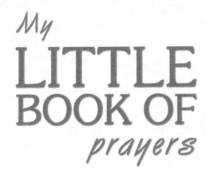

My
LITTLE
BOOK OF
prayers

Contents

Suffering

Guidance

Comfort

The Lord's prayer

Our Father who art in heaven,
　　hallowed be Your name,
　　Your kingdom come,
　　Your will be done
　　on earth as it is in heaven.
Give us today our daily bread.
Forgive us our trespasses,
　　as we forgive those
　　who trespass against us.
Lead us not into temptation,
　　but deliver us from evil.
For Yours is the kingdom,
　　and the power and the glory
　　for ever and ever.

　　Amen.

Jesus

Spiritual Intimacy

Day by day

Thanks be to Thee,
Lord Jesus Christ,

for all the benefits
which Thou hast won for us,

for all the pains and insults
which Thou hast borne for us.

O most merciful Redeemer,
Friend and Brother,

may we know Thee more clearly,
love Thee more dearly,

and follow Thee more nearly,
day by day.

Richard of Chichester

Spiritual Intimacy

The wisdom of God

I praise Thee, O God, for illuminating my mind and for enabling me to prove demonstratively that Thy wisdom is as infinite as Thy power. Help me to use these discoveries to praise and love and obey, and may I be exceedingly careful that my affections keep pace with my knowledge.

Help me to be not too curious in prying into those secret things that are known only to Thee, O God. May I not perplex myself about those methods of Providence that seem to me involved and intricate, but resolve them into Thine infinite wisdom, who knowest the spirit of all flesh and dost best understand how to govern those souls Thou hast created.

Thy boundless mind comprehends, at one view, all things, past, present and future, and Thou dost see all things, Thou dost best understand what is good and proper for each individual and for me.

Susannah Wesley

Desire for God

O Lord our God,
grant us grace
to desire You
with our whole heart,

that so desiring
we may seek
and find You,

and so finding You,
may love You,

and loving You,
may hate those sins
from which You have
redeemed us.

Anselm

In Christ's footsteps

The prayers I make will then be sweet indeed
if Thou the spirit give by which I pray.
My unassisted heart is barren clay,
that of its native self can nothing feed,
of good and pious works Thou art the seed
that quickens only where Thou say'st it may.

Unless Thou show to us Thine own true way
no man can find it: Father!
Thou must lead.
Do Thou, then, breathe
those thoughts into my mind
by which such virtue may in me be bred,
that in Thy holy footsteps I may tread;
the fetters of my tongue do Thou unbind
that I may have the power to sing of Thee
and sound Thy praises everlastingly.

Michelangelo Buonarroti

Spiritual Intimacy

A covenant of love

O LORD, God of Israel,
   there is no God like you in heaven above or
   on earth below – you who keep your covenant
   of love with your servants
   who continue wholeheartedly in your way.
Hear the cry and the prayer
   that your servant is praying in your presence
   this day.
May your eyes be open toward this temple
   night and day,
   this place of which you said,
   'My Name shall be there,'
   so that you will hear the prayer your servant
   prays toward this place.
Hear from heaven, your dwelling place,
   and when you hear, forgive.

1 Kings 8:23, 28-30

Solomon

Spiritual Intimacy

To know Christ

I keep asking that the God of our Lord Jesus Christ,
the glorious Father,
    may give you the Spirit of wisdom
    and revelation,
    so that you may know him better.
I pray also that the eyes of your heart
    may be enlightened
    in order that you may know the hope
    to which he has called you,
    the riches of his glorious inheritance
    in the saints,
    and his incomparably great power
    for us who believe.

Ephesians 1:17-19

Paul

Spiritual Intimacy

Jesus – desire of hungry hearts

O Jesu, the light and brightness of everlasting glory, the joy and comfort of all Christian people that are walking and laboring in the wilderness of this world, my heart crieth to Thee by still desires without voice and my silence speaketh unto Thee – Come, Lord, come, for without Thee I have no glad day nor hour, for Thou art all my joy and without Thee my soul is barren and void. I will not cease of prayer till Thy grace return to me again, and Thou speak inwardly to my soul and say thus, "Lo, I am here come to thee, for thou hast called Me. Thy tears and the desire of thy heart, thy meekness and thy contrition have brought me to thee."

There is none like to Thee, Lord, in heaven or in earth. Thy works be good. Thy judgments be righteous, and by Thy providence all things be governed. Wherefore to Thee, who art the Wisdom of the Father, be everlasting joy and glory.

Thomas à Kempis

Jesus – joy of loving hearts

Jesus, Thou joy of loving hearts,
    Thou fount of life, Thou light of men,
From the best bliss that earth imparts
    We turn unfilled to Thee again.

Our restless spirits yearn for Thee,
    Where'er our changeful lot is cast -
Glad when Thy gracious smile we see,
    Blest when our faith can hold Thee fast.

O Jesus, ever with us stay;
    Make all our moments calm and bright;
Chase the dark night of sin away,
    Shed o'er the world Thy holy light.

Bernard of Clairvaux

Spiritual Intimacy

God's love

I pray that out of his glorious riches
    he may strengthen you with power
    through his Spirit in your inner being,
    so that Christ may dwell in your hearts
    through faith.
And I pray that you,
    being rooted and established in love,
    may have power, together with all the saints,
    to grasp how wide and long and high and deep
    is the love of Christ,
    and to know this love
    that surpasses knowledge –
    that you may be filled to the measure
    of all the fullness of God.

Ephesians 3:16-19

Paul

The Way, the Truth and the Life

O Lord Jesus Christ,
You have said
that You are

the way,
the truth,
and the life.

Suffer us not
to stray from You,
who are the way,

nor to distrust You,
who are the truth,

nor to rest in anything
other than You,
who are the life.

Desiderius Erasmus

Spiritual Intimacy

Contemplating the nature of God

O Absolute Sovereign of the world! Thou art Supreme Omnipotence, Sovereign Goodness, Wisdom itself! Thou art without beginning and without end. Thy works are limitless, Thy perfections infinite, and Thy intelligence is supreme! Thou art a fathomless abyss of marvels. O Beauty, containing all other beauty! O great God, Thou art Strength itself.

Would that I possessed at this moment all the combined eloquence and wisdom of men! Then, in as far as it is possible here below, where knowledge is so limited, I could strive to make known one of Thy innumerable perfections. The contemplation of these reveals to some extent the nature of Him who is our Lord and our only God.

Teresa of Avila

Seek His face

One thing I ask of the LORD, this is what I seek: that I may dwell in the house of the LORD all the days of my life, to gaze upon the beauty of the LORD and to seek him in his temple.

For in the day of trouble he will keep me safe in his dwelling; he will hide me in the shelter of his tabernacle and set me high upon a rock.

Then my head will be exalted above the enemies who surround me; at his tabernacle will I sacrifice with shouts of joy; I will sing and make music to the LORD. Hear my voice when I call, O LORD; be merciful to me and answer me.

My heart says of you, "Seek his face!" Your face, LORD, I will seek. Do not hide your face from me, do not turn your servant away in anger; you have been my helper. Do not reject me or forsake me, O God my Savior.

Psalm 27:4-9

David

Spiritual Intimacy

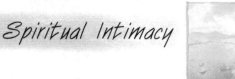

A heart of love

Lord, when my eye confronts my heart, and I realize that you have filled my heart with your love, I am breathless with amazement.

Once my heart was so small in its vision, so narrow in its compassion, so weak in its zeal for truth. Then you chose to enter my heart, and now in my heart I can see you, I can love all your people, and I have courage to proclaim the truth of your gospel to anyone and everyone.

Like wax before a fire, my heart has melted under the heat of your love.

Count Von Zinzendorf

How majestic is Your name

O LORD, our Lord, how majestic is your name in all the earth! You have set your glory above the heavens. From the lips of children and infants you have ordained praise because of your enemies, to silence the foe and the avenger.

When I consider your heavens, the work of your fingers, the moon and the stars, which you have set in place, what is man that you are mindful of him, the son of man that you care for him?

You made him a little lower than the heavenly beings and crowned him with glory and honor.

You made him ruler over the works of your hands; you put everything under his feet: all flocks and herds, and the beasts of the field, the birds of the air, and the fish of the sea, all that swim the paths of the seas. O LORD, our Lord, how majestic is your name in all the earth!

Psalm 8

David

Praise

The Lord is great

No one is like you, O LORD;
    you are great,
    and your name is mighty
    in power.
Who should not revere you,
    O King of the nations?
    This is your due.
Among all the wise men
    of the nations
    and in all their kingdoms,
    there is no one like you.
But the LORD is the true God;
    he is the living God,
    the eternal King.

Jeremiah 10:6-7, 10

Jeremiah

Prayer of exaltation

Blessed be your glorious name,
    and may it be exalted
    above all blessing and praise.
You alone are the LORD.
You made the heavens,
    even the highest heavens,
    and all their starry host,
    the earth and all that is on it,
    the seas and all that is in them.
You give life to everything,
    and the multitudes of heaven worship you.
You have kept your promise
    because you are righteous.

Nehemiah 9:5-6, 8

The Levites

Holy, holy, holy

Holy, holy, holy
   is the Lord God Almighty,
   who was, and is, and is to come.
You are worthy, our Lord and God,
   to receive glory and honor and power,
   for you created all things,
   and by your will they were created
   and have their being.
You are worthy to take the scroll
   and to open its seals, because you were slain,
   and with your blood you purchased men
   for God from every tribe and language
   and people and nation.
You have made them to be a kingdom and priests
   to serve our God,
   and they will reign on the earth.

Revelation 4:8, 11; 5:9-10

Twenty-four elders

The Lord our Maker

I praise you because I am fearfully
  and wonderfully made;
  your works are wonderful, I know that full well.
My frame was not hidden from you
  when I was made in the secret place.
When I was woven together
  in the depths of the earth,
  your eyes saw my unformed body.
All the days ordained for me
  were written in your book
  before one of them came to be.
How precious to me are your thoughts,
  O God! How vast is the sum of them!
Were I to count them,
  they would outnumber the grains of sand.
When I awake,
  I am still with you.

Psalm 139:14-18

David

Our cup of happiness

Lord God, how full our cup of happiness!
We drink and drink – and yet it grows not less;
But every morn the newly risen sun
Finds it replenished, sparkling, overrun.
Hast Thou not given us raiment,
warmth and meat,
And in due season, all earth's fruits to eat?
Work for our hands and rainbows for our eyes,
And for our souls the wings of butterflies?
A father's smile, a mother's fond embrace,
The tender light upon a lover's face?
The talk of friends, the twinkling eye of mirth,
The whispering silence of the good green earth?
Hope for our youth and memories for age,
And psalms upon the heaven's moving page?
And dost Thou not of pain a mingling pour,
To make the cup but overflow the more?

Gilbert Thomas

Let everything that has breath ...

All you big things, bless the Lord.
Mount Kilimanjaro and Lake Victoria,
The Rift Valley and the Serengeti Plain,
Fat baobabs and shady mango trees,
All eucalyptus and tamarind trees,
Bless the Lord.
Praise and extol Him
forever and ever.

All you tiny things, bless the Lord.
Busy black ants and hopping fleas,
Wriggling tadpoles and mosquito larvae,
Flying locusts and water drops,
Pollen dust and tsetse flies,
Millet seeds and dried corn,
Bless the Lord.
Praise and extol Him
forever and ever.

Traditional African verse

Song of thanksgiving

Praise be to you, O Lord,
    God of our father Israel,
    from everlasting to everlasting.
Yours, O Lord,
    is the greatness and the power and the glory
    and the majesty and the splendor,
    for everything in heaven and earth is yours.
Yours, O Lord, is the kingdom;
    you are exalted as head over all.
Wealth and honor come from you;
    you are the ruler of all things.
In your hands are strength and power
    to exalt and give strength to all.
Now, our God, we give you thanks,
    and praise your glorious name.

1 Chronicles 29:10-13

David

God's faithfulness

Listen, O heavens, and I will speak;
   hear, O earth, the words of my mouth.
Let my teaching fall like rain
   and my words descend like dew,
   like showers on new grass,
   like abundant rain on tender plants.

I will proclaim the name of the LORD.
   Oh, praise the greatness of our God!
He is the Rock, his works are perfect,
   and all his ways are just.
A faithful God who does no wrong,
   upright and just is he.

Deuteronomy 32:1-4

Moses

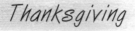

The Lord triumphs

I will sing to the LORD, for he is highly exalted.

The LORD is my strength and my song; he has become my salvation. He is my God, and I will praise him, my father's God, and I will exalt him.

The LORD is a warrior; the LORD is his name. Your right hand, O LORD, was majestic in power.

Who among the gods is like you, O LORD? Who is like you – majestic in holiness, awesome in glory, working wonders?

In your unfailing love you will lead the people you have redeemed. In your strength you will guide them to your holy dwelling.

You will bring them in and plant them on the mountain of your inheritance – the place, O LORD, you made for your dwelling, the sanctuary, O Lord, your hands established.

The LORD will reign for ever and ever.

Exodus 15:1-3, 6, 11, 13, 17-18

Moses

My heart rejoices

My heart rejoices in the LORD. There is no one holy like the LORD; there is no one besides you; there is no Rock like our God, for the LORD is a God who knows, and by him deeds are weighed.

The bows of the warriors are broken, but those who stumbled are armed with strength. Those who were full hire themselves out for food, but those who were hungry hunger no more. She who was barren has borne seven children, but she who has had many sons pines away.

The LORD brings death and makes alive; he brings down to the grave and raises up. The LORD sends poverty and wealth; he humbles and he exalts. He raises the poor from the dust and lifts the needy from the ash heap. For the foundations of the earth are the LORD's; upon them he has set the world. He will guard the feet of his saints.

1 Samuel 2:1-9

Hannah

Thanksgiving

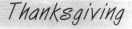

The glory of the Lord

How many are your works, O LORD!
   In wisdom you made them all;
    the earth is full of your creatures.
These all look to you
   to give them their food at the proper time.
When you give it to them,
   they gather it up; when you open your hand,
   they are satisfied with good things.
May the glory of the LORD endure forever;
   may the LORD rejoice in his works.
I will sing to the LORD all my life;
   I will sing praise to my God as long as I live.

Psalm 104:24, 27-28, 31, 33

Unknown

A song of thanks

I will praise you, O LORD, with all my heart;
    before the "gods" I will sing your praise.
I will bow down toward your holy temple
    and will praise your name
    for your love and your faithfulness,
    for you have exalted above all things
    your name and your word.
When I called, you answered me;
    you made me bold and stouthearted.
May all the kings of the earth praise you,
    O LORD, when they hear the words of your
    mouth.
May they sing of the ways of the LORD,
    for the glory of the LORD is great.
The LORD will fulfill his purpose for me;
    your love, O LORD, endures forever – do not
    abandon the works of your hands.

Psalm 138:1-5; 8

David

Confession

General confession

Almighty and most merciful Father, we have erred and strayed from thy ways like lost sheep.

We have followed too much the devices of our own hearts; we have left undone those things which we ought to have done; and we have done those things which we ought not to have done; and there is no health in us.

But, Thou, O Lord have mercy upon us miserable offenders; spare Thou those, O God, who confess their faults, restore Thou those who are penitent according to Thy promises declared unto mankind in Christ Jesus Our Lord; and grant, O most merciful Father, for His sake that we may hereafter live a godly, righteous and sober life, to the glory of Thy holy name.

Book of Common Prayer

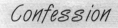

Confession

Collect for Lent

Almighty and everlasting God,
   You hate nothing
   that You have made,
   and forgive the sins of all those
   who are penitent.

Create and make in us new
   and contrite hearts,
   that, lamenting our sins
   and acknowledging our
   wretchedness,
   we may receive from You,
   the God of all mercy,
   perfect forgiveness
   and peace;
   through Jesus Christ
   our Lord

   Amen.

Thomas Cranmer

Confession

Prayer of repentance

Have mercy on me, O God,
   according to your unfailing love;
   according to your great compassion
   blot out my transgressions.
Wash away all my iniquity
   and cleanse me from my sin.

Create in me a pure heart, O God,
   and renew a steadfast spirit within me.
Do not cast me from your presence
   or take your Holy Spirit from me.
Restore to me the joy of your salvation
   and grant me a willing spirit, to sustain me.
 Then I will teach transgressors your ways,
   and sinners will turn back to you.

Psalm 51:1-2, 10-13

David

Confession

A prayer of the backslider

Although our sins testify against us,
O LORD, do something
for the sake of your name.
For our backsliding is great,
we have sinned against you.
You are among us, O LORD,
and we bear your name;
do not forsake us!

Jeremiah 14:7, 9

Jeremiah

~

Father, I have sinned against
heaven and against you.

Luke 15:18

The Prodigal Son

Confession

Prayer for forgiveness

Who is a God like you,
   who pardons sin and
   forgives the transgression
   of the remnant of his inheritance?
You do not stay angry forever
   but delight to show mercy.
You will again have compassion on us;
   you will tread our sins underfoot
   and hurl all our iniquities
   into the depths of the sea.

Micah 7:18-19

Micah

Job's confession

I know that you can do all things;
    no plan of yours can be thwarted.
You asked, 'Who is this that obscures my counsel
    without knowledge?'
Surely I spoke of things I did not understand,
    things too wonderful for me to know.
You said, 'Listen now, and I will speak;
    I will question you, and you shall answer me.'
My ears had heard of you
    but now my eyes have seen you.
Therefore I despise myself
    and repent in dust and ashes.

Job 42:2-6

Job

Confession

A prayer for restoration

Remember, O Lord, what has happened to us;
  look, and see our disgrace.
Joy is gone from our hearts;
  our dancing has turned to mourning.
The crown has fallen from our head.
  Woe to us, for we have sinned!
Because of this our hearts are faint,
  because of these things our eyes grow dim.
You, O Lord, reign forever; your throne endures
  from generation to generation.
Why do you always forget us?
  Why do you forsake us so long?
Restore us to yourself, O Lord,
  that we may return; renew our days as of old
  unless you have utterly rejected us
  and are angry with us beyond measure.

Lamentations 5:1, 15-17, 19-22

Jeremiah

The shame of guilt

O my God, I am too ashamed and disgraced to lift up my face to you, my God, because our sins are higher than our heads and our guilt has reached to the heavens. From the days of our forefathers until now, our guilt has been great.

But now, for a brief moment, the LORD our God has been gracious in leaving us a remnant and giving us a firm place in his sanctuary, and so our God gives light to our eyes and a little relief in our bondage.

What has happened to us is a result of our evil deeds and our great guilt, and yet, our God, you have punished us less than our sins have deserved. O LORD, God of Israel, you are righteous! We are left this day as a remnant. Here we are before you in our guilt, though because of it not one of us can stand in your presence.

Ezra 9:6-8, 13-15

Ezra

Times of trouble

Cry of the needy

Hasten, O God, to save me;
   O Lord, come quickly to help me.
May those who seek my life
   be put to shame and confusion;
   may all who desire my ruin
   be turned back in disgrace.
May those who say to me, "Aha! Aha!"
   turn back because of their shame.
But may all who seek you
   rejoice and be glad in you;
   may those who love your salvation always say,
   "Let God be exalted!"
Yet I am poor and needy;
   come quickly to me, O God.
You are my help and my deliverer;
   O Lord, do not delay.

Psalm 70:1-5

David

Steadfastness

O merciful God, be Thou unto me a strong tower of defence I humbly entreat Thee.

Give me grace to await Thy leisure and patiently to bear what Thou doest unto me; nothing doubting or mistrusting Thy goodness towards me: for Thou knowest what is good for me better than I do.

Therefore do with me in all things what Thou wilt; only arm me, I beseech Thee with Thine armor that I may stand fast; above all things, taking to me the shield of faith; praying always that I may refer myself wholly to Thy will, abiding Thy pleasure and comforting myself in those troubles which it shall please Thee to send to me, seeing such troubles are profitable for me; and I am assuredly persuaded that all Thou doest cannot but be well.

And unto Thee be all honor and glory.

Lady Jane Grey

Times of trouble

A prayer when facing sickness

Lord, whose spirit is so good and so gentle in all things, and who art so compassionate that not only all prosperity but even all afflictions that come to Thine elect are the results of Thy compassion.

Grant me grace that I may not do as the pagans do in the condition to which Thy justice has reduced me; grant that as a true Christian, I may recognize Thee as my Father and as my God in whatever estate I find myself, since the change in my condition brings no change in Thine own ...

Grant then, Lord, that I may conform to Thy will, just as I am, that being sick as I am, I may glorify Thee in my sufferings.

Blaise Pascal

Job's lament

I will say to God: Do not condemn me,
    but tell me what charges you have against me.
Does it please you to oppress me,
    to spurn the work of your hands,
    while you smile on the schemes of the wicked?
Do you have eyes of flesh?
Do you see as a mortal sees?
Are your days like those of a mortal
    or your years like those of a man,
    that you must search out my faults
    and probe after my sin –
    though you know that I am not guilty
    and that no one can rescue me from your hand?
Your hands shaped me and made me.
Will you now turn and destroy me?

Job 10:2-8

Job

Prayer in crisis

O Lord Almighty, God of Israel, enthroned between the cherubim, you alone are God over all the kingdoms of the earth. You have made heaven and earth.

Give ear, O Lord, and hear; open your eyes, O Lord, and see; listen to all the words Sennacherib has sent to insult the living God.

It is true, O Lord, that the Assyrian kings have laid waste all these peoples and their lands.

They have thrown their gods into the fire and destroyed them, for they were not gods but only wood and stone, fashioned by human hands.

Now, O Lord our God, deliver us from his hand, so that all kingdoms on earth may know that you alone, O Lord, are God.

Isaiah 37:16-20

Hezekiah

What can man do to me?

Be merciful to me, O God,
   for men hotly pursue me;
   all day long they press their attack.
My slanderers pursue me all day long;
   many are attacking me in their pride.
When I am afraid, I will trust in you.
   In God, whose word I praise,
   in God I trust; I will not be afraid.
What can mortal man do to me?
Record my lament; list my tears on your scroll
   – are they not in your record?
Then my enemies will turn back when I call for help.
By this I will know that God is for me.
For you have delivered me from death
   and my feet from stumbling,
   that I may walk before God in the light of life.

Psalm 56:1-4; 8-9; 13

David

Times of trouble

Refuge for the upright

In you, O LORD, I have taken refuge; let me never be put to shame.

Rescue me and deliver me in your righteousness; turn your ear to me and save me.

Be my rock of refuge, to which I can always go; give the command to save me, for you are my rock and my fortress.

Deliver me, O my God, from the hand of the wicked, from the grasp of evil and cruel men.

For you have been my hope, O Sovereign LORD, my confidence since my youth.

From birth I have relied on you; you brought me forth from my mother's womb. I will ever praise you.

My mouth is filled with your praise, declaring your splendor all day long.

Psalm 71:1-6, 8

David

Cry for mercy

To you I call, O LORD my Rock;
    do not turn a deaf ear to me.
For if you remain silent,
    I will be like those who have gone down
    to the pit.
Hear my cry for mercy
    as I call to you for help,
    as I lift up my hands
    toward your Most Holy Place.
Praise be to the LORD,
    for he has heard my cry for mercy.
The LORD is my strength and my shield;
    my heart trusts in him, and I am helped.
My heart leaps for joy
    and I will give thanks to him in song.

Psalm 28:1-2, 6-7

David

Times of trouble

Overtaken by troubles

Do not withhold your mercy from me, O Lord; may your love and your truth always protect me.

For troubles without number surround me; my sins have overtaken me, and I cannot see. They are more than the hairs of my head, and my heart fails within me.

Be pleased, O Lord, to save me; O Lord, come quickly to help me.

May all who seek to take my life be put to shame and confusion; may all who desire my ruin be turned back in disgrace.

May those who say to me, "Aha! Aha!" be appalled at their own shame.

But may all who seek you rejoice and be glad in you; may those who love your salvation always say, "The Lord be exalted!"

Psalm 40:11-16

David

Prayer of the afflicted

For the sake of your name, O LORD, forgive my iniquity, though it is great.

Turn to me and be gracious to me, for I am lonely and afflicted.

The troubles of my heart have multiplied; free me from my anguish.

Look upon my affliction and my distress and take away all my sins.

See how my enemies have increased and how fiercely they hate me!

Guard my life and rescue me; let me not be put to shame, for I take refuge in you.

May integrity and uprightness protect me, because my hope is in you.

Psalm 25:11, 16-21

David

Times of trouble

Light in the darkness

The LORD has rewarded me according to my righteousness, according to my cleanness in his sight.

To the faithful you show yourself faithful, to the blameless you show yourself blameless, to the pure you show yourself pure, but to the crooked you show yourself shrewd.

You save the humble, but your eyes are on the haughty to bring them low.

You are my lamp, O LORD; the LORD turns my darkness into light.

With your help I can advance against a troop; with my God I can scale a wall.

As for God, his way is perfect; the word of the LORD is flawless. He is a shield for all who take refuge in him.

2 Samuel 22:25-31

David

Open my eyes ...

O Lord, open my eyes
  that I may see the needs of others;
  open my ears that I may hear their cries;
  open my heart so that they need not be
  without succor;
  let me not be afraid to defend the weak
  because of the anger of the strong,
  nor be afraid to defend the poor
  because of the anger of the rich.
Show me where love and hope and faith
  are needed,
  and use me to bring them to those places.
And so open my eyes and ears
  that I may this coming day be able to do some
  work of peace for Thee.
  Amen

Alan Paton

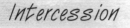

Protection for children

Father, hear us, we are praying
    hear the words our hearts are saying,
    we are praying for our children.
Keep them from the powers of evil,
    from the secret, hidden peril,
    from the whirlpool that would suck them,
    from the treacherous quicksand pluck them.
From the worldling's hollow gladness,
    from the sting of faithless sadness,
    Holy Father, save our children.
Through life's troubled waters steer them, through
life's bitter battle cheer them,
    Father, Father, be Thou near them.
Read the language of our longing,
    read the wordless pleadings thronging,
    Holy Father, for our children.
And wherever they may hide,
    lead them Home at eventide.

Amy Carmichael

Spirit of intercession

Lord, save us from being self-centered
   in our prayers,
   and teach us to remember to pray for others.
May we be so bound up in love with those
   for whom we pray
   that we may feel their needs
   as acutely as our own
   and intercede for them with sensitivity,
   with understanding,
   and with imagination.
We ask this in Christ's name.

John Calvin

Fruit of righteousness

I thank my God every time I remember you. In all my prayers for all of you, I always pray with joy because of your partnership in the gospel from the first day until now, being confident of this, that he who began a good work in you will carry it on to completion until the day of Christ Jesus.

And this is my prayer: that your love may abound more and more in knowledge and depth of insight, so that you may be able to discern what is best and may be pure and blameless until the day of Christ, filled with the fruit of righteousness that comes through Jesus Christ – to the glory and praise of God.

Philippians 1:3-6, 9-11

Paul

Bearing fruit

For this reason, since the day we heard about you, we have not stopped praying for you and asking God to fill you with the knowledge of his will through all spiritual wisdom and understanding.

And we pray this in order that you may live a life worthy of the Lord and may please him in every way: bearing fruit in every good work, growing in the knowledge of God, being strengthened with all power according to his glorious might so that you may have great endurance and patience, and joyfully giving thanks to the Father, who has qualified you to share in the inheritance of the saints in the kingdom of light.

Colossians 1:9-12

Paul

Spiritual riches

O Jesus, Son of God, carpenter of Nazareth,
  grant sight to those blinded by luxury
  and deliverance to those bound by want,
  that the rich may joyfully follow the simplicity
  of thy most holy life,
  and the poor may obtain their inheritance,
  and that the hearts of all may be set
  with one accord
  to discover the way of salvation,
  through Thy mercy
  who for our sake didst become poor
  that we, through Thy poverty,
  might become rich.
  And this we ask for Thy name's sake.
  Amen.

Unknown

For the preaching of the gospel

Almighty and everlasting God, save us from all error, ignorance, pride and prejudice; and of Thy great mercy vouchsafe, we beseech Thee, so to direct, sanctify and govern us in our work, by the mighty power of the Holy Spirit, that the comfortable Gospel of Christ may be truly preached, truly received, and truly followed in all places to the breaking down of the kingdom of sin, Satan and death; till at length the whole of Thy dispersed sheep, being gathered into Thy fold, shall become partakers of everlasting life, through the merits and death of Jesus Christ our Savior.

Amen

Book of Common Prayer

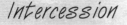

Intercession

Moses intercedes for the Israelites

The next day Moses said to the people,
   "You have committed a great sin.
   But now I will go up to the LORD;
   perhaps I can make atonement for your sin."
So Moses went back to the LORD and said,
   "Oh, what a great sin
   these people have committed!
   They have made themselves gods of gold.
But now, please forgive their sin –
   but if not,
   then blot me out
   of the book you have written."

Exodus 32:30-32

Moses

Evening prayer

Go with each of us to rest;
   if any awake, temper to them
   the dark hours of watching;
   and when the day returns, return to us,
   our Sun and Comforter,
   and call us up with morning faces
   and with morning hearts,
   eager to labor,
   eager to be happy,
   if happiness should be our portion,
   and if the day be marked for sorrow,
   strong to endure it.

Robert Louis Stevenson

Surrender

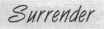

Covenant blessings

Eternal Father, it is amazing love that Thou hast sent Thy Son to suffer in my stead, that Thou hast added the Spirit to teach, comfort and guide, that Thou hast allowed the ministry of angels to wall me round.

Arise to my help in richness of covenant blessings, keep me feeding in the pastures of Thy strengthening Word, searching Scriptures to find Thee there.

Let all Thy Fatherly dealings make me a partaker of Thy holiness. Grant that in every fall I may sink lower on my knees, and that when I rise it may be to loftier heights of devotion.

May my every cross be sanctified, every loss be gain, every denial a spiritual advantage, every dark day a light of the Holy Spirit, every night of trial of song.

Puritan Prayer

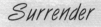

Dedication

Teach us, Lord,
    to serve You as You deserve,
    to give and not to count the cost,
    to fight and not to heed the wounds,
    to toil and not to seek for rest,
    to labor and not to ask for any reward
    save that of knowing that we do Your will.

Ignatius of Loyola

Surrender

Prayer of relinquishment

Though the fig tree does not bud
  and there are no grapes on the vines,
  though the olive crop fails
  and the fields produce no food,
  though there are no sheep in the pen
  and no cattle in the stalls,
  yet I will rejoice in the LORD,
  I will be joyful in God my Savior.

Habakkuk 3:17-18

Habakkuk

An example of a godly life

Oh that the things which were seen and heard in this extraordinary person; his holiness, labor and self-denial in life; his heart and practice to the glory of God; and the wonderful frame of mind manifested in so steadfast a manner, under the expectation of death, and under the pains and agonies which brought it on; may excite in us all, both ministers and people, a due sense of the greatness of the work which we have to do in the world, of the excellency and amiableness of thorough religion in experience and practice, of the blessedness of the end of those whose death finishes such a life, and of the infinite value of their eternal reward ... and effectually stir us up to constant endeavors that, in the way of such a holy life, we may at last come to as blessed an end!

Amen

Jonathan Edwards

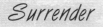

The Potter and the clay

Since ancient times no one has heard, no ear has perceived, no eye has seen any God besides you, who acts on behalf of those who wait for him.

You come to the help of those who gladly do right, who remember your ways. But when we continued to sin against them, you were angry. How then can we be saved?

All of us have become like one who is unclean.

Yet, O LORD, you are our Father. We are the clay, you are the potter; we are all the work of your hand.

Do not be angry beyond measure, O LORD; do not remember our sins forever. Oh, look upon us, we pray, for we are all your people.

Isaiah 64:4-6, 8-9

Isaiah

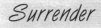

Prayer of surrender

Naked I came from my mother's womb,
and naked I will depart.
The LORD gave
and the LORD has taken away;
may the name of the Lord
be praised.

Job 1:21

Job

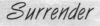

Surrender

Prayer of consecration

What more can David say to you for honoring your servant? For you know your servant, O LORD. For the sake of your servant and according to your will, you have done this great thing and made known all these great promises.

There is no one like you, O LORD, and there is no God but you, as we have heard with our own ears.

And now, LORD, let the promise you have made concerning your servant and his house be established forever. Do as you promised, so that it will be established and that your name will be great forever. Then men will say, 'The LORD Almighty, the God over Israel, is Israel's God!' And the house of your servant David will be established before you.

1 Chronicles 17:18-20; 23-24

David

Song of Simeon (Nunc Dimittis)

"Sovereign Lord, as you have promised,
   you now dismiss your servant in peace.
For my eyes have seen your salvation,
   which you have prepared
   in the sight of all people,
   a light for revelation to the Gentiles
   and for glory to your people Israel."
The child's father and mother marveled at what
was said about him.
Then Simeon blessed them and said to Mary, his
mother:
   "This child is destined to cause the falling and
   rising of many in Israel,
   and to be a sign that will be spoken against,
   so that the thoughts of many hearts
   will be revealed.
   And a sword will pierce your own soul too."

Luke 2:29-35

Simeon

Surrender

Jesus' anguish in Gethsemane

They went to a place called Gethsemane, and Jesus said to his disciples, "Sit here while I pray."

He took Peter, James and John along with him, and he began to be deeply distressed and troubled.

"My soul is overwhelmed with sorrow to the point of death," he said to them. "Stay here and keep watch."

Going a little farther, he fell to the ground and prayed that if possible the hour might pass from him.

"*Abba*, Father," he said, "everything is possible for you. Take this cup from me. Yet not what I will, but what you will."

Mark 14:32-36

Jesus

Take my life

Take my life and let it be
consecrated, Lord, to Thee,
take my moments and my days;
let them flow in ceaseless praise.

Take my will and make it Thine;
it shall be no longer mine.
Take my heart – it is Thine own;
it shall be Thy royal throne.

Take my love; my Lord, I pour
at Thy feet its treasure-store.
Take myself and I will be
ever, only, all for Thee!

Frances Ridley Havergal

Suffering

Prayer in captivity

In me there is darkness, but with You there is light; I am lonely, but You do not leave me; I am feeble in heart, but with You there is help; I am restless, but with You there is peace.

In me there is bitterness, but with You there is patience; I do not understand Your ways, but You know the way for me.

Lord Jesus Christ, You were poor and in distress, a captive and forsaken as I am.

You know all man's troubles; You abide with me when all men fail me; You remember and seek me; it is Your will that I should know You and turn to You.

Lord, I hear Your call and follow; help me.

Dietrich Bonhoeffer

Relief from distress

Answer me when I call to you, O my righteous God. Give me relief from my distress; be merciful to me and hear my prayer.

How long, O men, will you turn my glory into shame? How long will you love delusions and seek false gods?

Know that the LORD has set apart the godly for himself; the LORD will hear when I call to him.

In your anger do not sin; when you are on your beds, search your hearts and be silent.

Let the light of your face shine upon us, O LORD.

You have filled my heart with greater joy than when their grain and new wine abound.

I will lie down and sleep in peace, for you alone, O LORD, make me dwell in safety.

Psalm 4:1-4; 6-8

David.

Suffering

Prayer for encouragement

May our Lord Jesus Christ himself and God our Father, who loved us and by his grace gave us eternal encouragement and good hope, encourage your hearts and strengthen you in every good deed and word.

Finally, brothers, pray for us that the message of the Lord may spread rapidly and be honored, just as it was with you. And pray that we may be delivered from wicked and evil men, for not everyone has faith. But the Lord is faithful, and he will strengthen and protect you from the evil one.

May the Lord direct your hearts into God's love and Christ's perseverance.

2 Thessalonians 2:16-17; 3:1-3, 5

Paul

A prayer for endurance

O Lord God when Thou givest to Thy servants
    to endeavor any great matter,
    grant us also to know
    that it is not the beginning
    but the continuing of the same,
    until it be thoroughly finished,
    which yieldeth the true glory;
    through Him that
    for the fininshing of Thy work
    laid down His life,
    our Redeemer Jesus Christ.

Sir Francis Drake

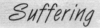
Suffering

A prayer when depressed

Answer me quickly, O LORD;
    my spirit fails.
Do not hide your face from me
    or I will be like those who go down to the pit.
Let the morning bring me word
    of your unfailing love,
        for I have put my trust in you.
Show me the way I should go,
    for to you I lift up my soul.
Rescue me from my enemies, O LORD,
    for I hide myself in you.
Teach me to do your will,
    for you are my God;
        may your good Spirit
        lead me on level ground.
For your name's sake, O LORD, preserve my life;
    in your righteousness, bring me out of trouble.

Psalm 143:7-11

David

When suffering rejection

My God, my God, why have you forsaken me? Why are you so far from saving me, so far from the words of my groaning? O my God, I cry out by day, but you do not answer, by night, and am not silent.

Yet you are enthroned as the Holy One; you are the praise of Israel. In you our fathers put their trust; they trusted and you delivered them. But I am a worm and not a man, scorned by men and despised by the people. All who see me mock me; they hurl insults, shaking their heads: He trusts in the LORD; let the LORD rescue him. Let him deliver him, since he delights in him.

Yet you brought me out of the womb; you made me trust in you even at my mother's breast. From birth I was cast upon you; from my mother's womb you have been my God.

Psalm 22:1-10

David

Suffering

The strength of the Lord

I love you, O LORD, my strength.

The LORD is my rock, my fortress and my deliverer; my God is my rock, in whom I take refuge. He is my shield and the horn of my salvation, my stronghold.

I call to the LORD, who is worthy of praise, and I am saved from my enemies.

In my distress I called to the LORD; I cried to my God for help. From his temple he heard my voice; my cry came before him, into his ears.

The LORD has rewarded me according to my righteousness, according to the cleanness of my hands in his sight.

To the faithful you show yourself faithful, to the blameless you show yourself blameless, to the pure you show yourself pure.

Psalm 18:1-3, 6, 24-26

David

A plea for justice

O LORD Almighty, you who judge righteously
    and test the heart and mind,
    let me see your vengeance upon them,
    for to you I have committed my cause.
You are always righteous, O LORD,
    when I bring a case before you.
Yet I would speak with you about your justice:
    Why does the way of the wicked prosper?
    Why do all the faithless live at ease?
You have planted them,
    and they have taken root;
    they grow and bear fruit.
You are always on their lips
    but far from their hearts.
Yet you know me, O LORD;
    you see me and test my thoughts about you.
Jeremiah 11:20, 12:1-3

Jeremiah

A cry for help

I call with all my heart; answer me, O LORD, and I will obey your decrees.

I call out to you; save me and I will keep your statutes.

I rise before dawn and cry for help; I have put my hope in your word.

My eyes stay open through the watches of the night, that I may meditate on your promises.

Hear my voice in accordance with your love; preserve my life, O LORD, according to your laws.

Those who devise wicked schemes are near, but they are far from your law.

Yet you are near, O LORD, and all your commands are true.

Long ago I learned from your statutes that you established them to last forever.

Psalm 119:145-152

The help of the Lord

Hasten, O God, to save me;
  O LORD, come quickly to help me.
May those who seek my life
  be put to shame and confusion;
  may all who desire my ruin
  be turned back in disgrace.
May those who say to me, "Aha! Aha!"
  turn back because of their shame.
But may all who seek you
  rejoice and be glad in you;
  may those who love your salvation always say,
  "Let God be exalted!"
Yet I am poor and needy;
  come quickly to me, O God.
You are my help and my deliverer;
  O LORD, do not delay.

Psalm 70:1-5

David

Guidance

Show me Your way ...

To you, O LORD, I lift up my soul; in you I trust, O my God. Do not let me be put to shame, nor let my enemies triumph over me.

No one whose hope is in you will ever be put to shame, but they will be put to shame who are treacherous without excuse.

Show me your ways, O LORD, teach me your paths; guide me in your truth and teach me, for you are God my Savior, and my hope is in you all day long.

Remember, O LORD, your great mercy and love, for they are from of old.

Remember not the sins of my youth and my rebellious ways; according to your love remember me, for you are good, O LORD.

Psalm 25:1-7

David

The Lord's purpose

When I called, you answered me;
   you made me bold and stouthearted.
Though the LORD is on high,
   he looks upon the lowly,
   but the proud he knows from afar.
Though I walk in the midst of trouble,
   you preserve my life;
   you stretch out your hand
   against the anger of my foes,
   with your right hand you save me.
The LORD will fulfill his purpose for me;
   your love, O LORD, endures forever –
   do not abandon the works of your hands.

Psalm 138:3, 6-8

David

Guidance

A prayer of sanction

O LORD, God of my master Abraham,
  give me success today,
  and show kindness to my master Abraham.
  See, I am standing beside this spring, and the
daughters of the townspeople are coming out to
draw water.
May it be that when I say to a girl,
  "Please let down your jar that I may have a
drink,"
  and she says, "Drink, and I'll water your cam-
els too" –
  let her be the one you have chosen for your
servant Isaac.
By this I will know that you have shown kindness
to my master.

Genesis 24:12-14

Abraham's servant

To walk in Your truth

Hear, O LORD, and answer me, for I am poor and needy. Guard my life, for I am devoted to you.

Bring joy to your servant, for to you, O Lord, I lift up my soul. You are forgiving and good, O Lord, abounding in love to all who call to you.

Hear my prayer, O LORD; listen to my cry for mercy. In the day of my trouble I will call to you, for you will answer me. For you are great and do marvelous deeds; you alone are God.

Teach me your way, O LORD, and I will walk in your truth; give me an undivided heart, that I may fear your name. I will praise you, O Lord my God, with all my heart; I will glorify your name forever. For great is your love toward me.

You, O Lord, are a compassionate and gracious God, slow to anger, abounding in love and faithfulness.

Psalm 86:1-2, 4-7; 10-13; 15

David

Guidance

The Lord leads ...

Who among the gods is like you, O LORD? Who is like you – majestic in holiness, awesome in glory, working wonders? You stretched out your right hand and the earth swallowed them. In your unfailing love you will lead the people you have redeemed.

In your strength you will guide them to your holy dwelling. The nations will hear and tremble. Terror and dread will fall upon them. By the power of your arm they will be as still as a stone – until your people pass by, O LORD, until the people you bought pass by.

You will bring them in and plant them on the mountain of your inheritance – the place, O LORD, you made for your dwelling, the sanctuary, O Lord, your hands established.

The LORD will reign for ever and ever.

Exodus 15:11-14; 16-18

Moses

A path through despair

How simple for me to live with You, Oh Lord. How easy for me to beleive in You! When my mind parts in bewilderment or falters, then the most intelligent people see no further than this day's end and do not know what must be done tomorrow. You grant me the serene certitude that You exist and that You will take care that not all the paths of good be closed.

Atop the ridge of earthly fame, I look back in wonder at the path which I alone could never have found, a wondrous path through despair to this point from which I, too, could transmit to mankind a reflection of Your rays. And as much as I must still reflect You will give me. But as much as I cannot take up You will have already assigned to others.

Alexander Solzhenitsyn

Guide me, O Thou great Jehovah

Guide me, O Thou great Jehovah;
pilgrim through this barren land;
I am weak, but Thou art mighty,
hold me with Thy powerful hand;
Bread of heaven, Bread of heaven,
feed me till I want no more,
feed me till I want no more.

Open Thou the crystal fountain,
whence the healing stream shall flow;
let the fiery, cloudy pillar
lead me all my journey through:
Strong deliverer, Strong deliverer
be Thou still my help and shield,
be Thou still my help and shield.

William Williams

Trees of righteousness

God of the gallant trees,
    give to us fortitude;
Give as Thou givest to these,
    valorous hardihood.
We are the trees of Thy planting, O God;
    we are the trees of Thy wood.

Now let the life-sap run
    clean through our every vein.
Perfect what Thou hast begun,
    God of the sun and rain,
Thou who dost measure
    the weight of the wind,
fit us for stress and for strain.

Amy Carmichael

A child learns to pray

Lord, teach a little child to pray,
    and then accept my prayer,
for Thou canst hear the words I say,
    for Thou art everywhere.

A little sparrow cannot fall
    unnoticed, Lord, by Thee;
and though I am so young and small,
    Thou dost take care of me.

Teach me to do the thing that's right,
    and when I sin, forgive;
and make it still my chief delight
    to serve Thee while I live.

Traditional

Persevere in the faith

We always thank God, the Father of our Lord Jesus Christ, when we pray for you, because we have heard of your faith in Christ Jesus and of the love you have for all the saints – the faith and love that spring from the hope that is stored up for you in heaven and that you have already heard about in the word of truth, the gospel that has come to you.

All over the world this gospel is bearing fruit and growing, just as it has been doing among you since the day you heard it and understood God's grace in all its truth.

Colossians 1:3-6

Paul

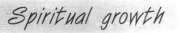

Teach us to pray

Lord, teach us to pray. Some of us are not skilled in the art of prayer. As we draw near to Thee in thought, our spirits long for Thy Spirit, and reach out for Thee, longing to feel Thee near. We know not how to express the deepest emotions that lie hidden in our hearts.

We would not be ignorant in prayer and, like children, only make want lists for Thee. Rather, we pray that Thou will give unto us only what we really need. We would not make our prayers the importuning of Thee, an omnipotent God, to do only what we want Thee to do. Rather, give us the vision, the courage, that shall enlarge our horizons and stretch our faith to the adventure of seeking Thy loving will for our lives.

We thank Thee that Thou art hearing us even now. We thank Thee for the grace of prayer. We thank Thee for Thyself.

Peter Marshall

Sanctification

I protected them and kept them safe by that name you gave me.

I say these things while I am still in the world, so that they may have the full measure of my joy within them.

I have given them your word and the world has hated them, for they are not of the world any more than I am of the world.

My prayer is not that you take them out of the world but that you protect them from the evil one. They are not of the world, even as I am not of it.

Sanctify them by the truth; your word is truth.

As you sent me into the world, I have sent them into the world.

For them I sanctify myself, that they too may be truly sanctified.

John 17:12-13, 14-19

Jesus

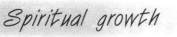

A pure heart

Give us
a pure heart,
    that we may see Thee
a humble heart,
    that we may hear Thee
a heart of love,
    that we may serve Thee
a heart of faith,
    that we may live Thee.
Thou whom I do not know, but Whose I am.
Thou whom I do not comprehend,
    but Who has dedicated me to my fate.
    Thou –
    Amen.

Dag Hammarskjold

A prayer of self-searching

O LORD, you have searched me
  and you know me.
You know when I sit
  and when I rise;
  you perceive my thoughts from afar.
You discern my going out
  and my lying down;
  you are familiar with all my ways.
Before a word is on my tongue
  you know it completely, O LORD.
Search me, O God,
  and know my heart;
  test me and know my anxious thoughts.
See if there is any offensive way in me,
  and lead me in the way everlasting.

Psalm 139:1-4;23-24

David

Unity of believers

My prayer is not for them alone.
I pray also for those who will believe in me
    through their message,
    that all of them may be one,
    Father, just as you are in me and I am in you.
May they also be in us
    so that the world may believe
    that you have sent me.
I have given them the glory that you gave me,
    that they may be one as we are one:
    I in them and you in me.
May they be brought to complete unity
    to let the world know that you sent me
    and have loved them
    even as you have loved me.

John 17:20-23

Jesus

Spiritual growth

Simplicity and joy

O Lord Christ,
   help us to maintain ourselves
   in simplicity and in joy,
   the joy of the merciful,
   the joy of brotherly love.

Grant that,
   renouncing henceforth
   all thought
   of looking back,
   and joyful with
   infinite gratitude,
   we may never fear to precede
   the dawn,
   to praise and bless
   and sing
   to Christ our Lord.

From the rule of Taizé

I would be true

I would be true, for there are those who trust me;
I would be pure, for there are those who care,
I would be strong, for there is much to suffer;
I would be brave, for there is much to dare.

I would be friend of all – the foe, the friendless,
I would be giving, and forget the gift.
I would be humble, for I know my weakness;
I would look up, and laugh, and love, and lift.

I would be prayerful, through each busy moment,
I would be constantly in touch with God.
I would be tuned to hear His slightest whisper;
I would have faith to keep the path Christ trod.

Howard Al Walter

Petition

Morning devotions

In the morning, O LORD, you hear my voice; in the morning I lay my requests before you and wait in expectation.

You are not a God who takes pleasure in evil; with you the wicked cannot dwell.

But I, by your great mercy, will come into your house; in reverence will I bow down toward your holy temple.

Lead me, O LORD, in your righteousness because of my enemies – make straight your way before me. Not a word from their mouth can be trusted; their heart is filled with destruction.

But let all who take refuge in you be glad; let them ever sing for joy. Spread your protection over them, that those who love your name may rejoice in you.

Psalm 5:3-4, 7-9, 11

David

Petition

Prayer of faith

Then Jesus said,
  "Did I not tell you that if you believed you
  would see the glory of God?"
Then Jesus looked up and said,
  "Father, I thank you that you have heard me.
  I knew that you always hear me, but I said this
for the benefit of the people standing here,
  that they may believe that you sent me."

John 11:40-42

Jesus

Prayer for favor

O LORD, God of heaven,
    the great and awesome God,
    who keeps his covenant of love with those who
love him and obey his commands,
    let your ear be attentive and your eyes open
    to hear the prayer your servant is praying
    before you day and night for your servants,
    the people of Israel.
O Lord, let your ear be attentive
    to the prayer of this your servant
    and to the prayer of your servants
    who delight in revering your name.
Give your servant success today
    by granting him favor
    in the presence of this man.

Nehemiah 1:5-6, 11

Nehemiah

Petition

The believers' prayer

Sovereign Lord, you made the heaven and the earth and the sea, and everything in them. You spoke by the Holy Spirit through the mouth of your servant, our father David: 'Why do the nations rage and the peoples plot in vain? The kings of the earth take their stand and the rulers gather together against the Lord and against his Anointed One.'

Indeed Herod and Pontius Pilate met together with the Gentiles and the people of Israel in this city to conspire against your holy servant Jesus, whom you anointed. They did what your power and will had decided beforehand should happen.

Now, Lord, consider their threats and enable your servants to speak your word with great boldness. Stretch out your hand to heal and perform miraculous signs and wonders through the name of your holy servant Jesus.

Acts 4:24-30

The believers

Jesus, Captain of my soul

O Lord of the oceans, my little bark sails on a restless sea, grant that Jesus may sit at the helm and steer me safely; suffer no adverse currents to divert my heaven ward course; let not my faith be wrecked amid storms and shoals.

Bring me to harbor with flying pennants, hull unbreached, cargo unspoiled.

I ask great things, expect great things, shall receive great things; I venture on Thee wholly, fully – my wind, sunshine, anchor and defense. May the world this day be happier and better because I live.

Let my mast before me be the Savior's cross, and every oncoming wave the fountain in His side.

Help me, protect me in the moving sea until I reach the shore of unceasing praise.

Traditional Puritan Prayer

Petition

Each day's need

Praise be to the LORD, who has given rest to his people Israel just as he promised. Not one word has failed of all the good promises he gave through his servant Moses. May the LORD our God be with us as he was with our fathers; may he never leave us nor forsake us. May he turn our hearts to him, to walk in all his ways and to keep the commands, decrees and regulations he gave our fathers.

And may these words of mine, which I have prayed before the LORD, be near to the LORD our God day and night, that he may uphold the cause of his servant and the cause of his people Israel according to each day's need, so that all the peoples of the earth may know that the LORD is God and that there is no other. But your hearts must be fully committed to the LORD our God, to live by his decrees and obey his commands, as at this time.

1 Kings 8:56-61

Solomon

Rest for the soul

I love the LORD, for he heard my voice;
  he heard my cry for mercy.
Because he turned his ear to me,
  I will call on him as long as I live.
The cords of death entangled me,
  the anguish of the grave came upon me;
  I was overcome by trouble and sorrow.
Then I called on the name of the LORD:
  "O LORD, save me!"
The LORD is gracious and righteous;
  our God is full of compassion.
The LORD protects the simplehearted;
  when I was in great need, he saved me.
Be at rest once more, O my soul,
  for the LORD has been good to you.

Psalm 116:1-7

Unknown

A righteous plea

Hear, O LORD, my righteous plea; listen to my cry. Give ear to my prayer – it does not rise from deceitful lips.

May my vindication come from you; may your eyes see what is right. Though you probe my heart and examine me at night, though you test me, you will find nothing; I have resolved that my mouth will not sin. By the word of your lips I have kept myself from the ways of the violent. My steps have held to your paths; my feet have not slipped.

I call on you, O God, for you will answer me; give ear to me and hear my prayer. Show the wonder of your great love, you who save by your right hand those who take refuge in you from their foes.

Keep me as the apple of your eye; hide me in the shadow of your wings from the wicked who assail me, from my mortal enemies who surround me.

Psalm 17:1-9

David

A mother's prayer

For all these smallnesses I thank You, Lord: small children and small needs; small meals to cook, small talk to heed, and a small book from which to read small stories; small hurts to heal, small disappointments, too, as real as ours; small glories to discover in bugs, pebbles, flowers.

When day is through my mind is small, my strength is gone; and as I gather each dear one I pray, "Bless each child for Jesus' sake – such angels sleeping, imps awake!"

What wears me out are little things: Angels minus shining wings.

Forgive me, Lord, if I have whined; it takes so much to keep them shined; yet each small rub has its reward, for they have blessed *me*.

Thank You, Lord.

Ruth Graham

Petition

Daily petition

Give me a good digestion, Lord,
　　and also something to digest;
　　give me a healthy body, Lord,
　　with sense to keep it at its best.
Give me a healthy mind, good Lord,
　　to keep the good and pure in sight,
　　which seeing sin is not appalled
　　but finds a way to set it right.
Give me a mind that is not bored,
　　that does not whimper, whine or sigh;
　　don't let me worry overmuch
　　about the fussy thing called I.
Give me a sense of humor, Lord,
　　give me the grace to see a joke,
　　to get some happiness from life
　　and pass it on to other folk.

Found in Chester Cathedral, England

Night watch

Watch, dear Lord, with those who wake,
    or watch, or weep tonight,
    and give Your angels charge
    over those who sleep.
Tend Your sick ones, O Lord Christ,
rest Your weary ones.
Bless Your dying ones.
Soothe Your suffering ones.
Pity Your afflicted ones.
Shield Your joyous ones.
And all for Your love's sake.
Amen.

Augustine of Hippo

Prayer of Jabez

Jabez cried out to the God of Israel,
  "Oh, that you would bless me
  and enlarge my territory!
Let your hand be with me,
  and keep me from harm
  so that I will be free from pain."

And God granted his request.

1 Chronicles 4:10

Jabez

Petition

Evening reflections

O Lord my God, thank You for bringing this day to a close; Thank You for giving me rest in body and soul.

Your hand has been over me and has guarded and preserved me.

Forgive my lack of faith and any wrong that I have done today, and help me to forgive all who have wronged me.

Let me sleep in peace under Your protection, and keep me from the temptations of darkness.

Into Your hands I commend my loved ones and all who dwell in this house; I commend to you my body and soul.

O God, Your holy name be praised.
Amen.

Dietrech Bonhoeffer

Petition

Abundant mercy

Almighty and everlasting God,
  who art always more ready to hear
  than we to pray,
  and art wont to give more than either we desire or deserve: Pour down upon us the abundance
of Thy mercy; forgiving us those things whereof
our conscience is afraid,
  and giving us those good things which we are
not worthy to ask,
  but through the merits and mediation of Jesus
Christ, Thy Son, our Lord.
  Amen.

Book of Common Prayer

The seasons of God's mercy

God, You made the sun and moon to distinguish seasons and day and night. And we cannot have the fruits of the earth but in their seasons. But You hath made no decree to distinguish the seasons of Your mercies. In Paradise the fruits were ripe the first minute, and in Heaven it is always autumn. Your mercies are ever in their maturity. You never say we should have come yesterday. You never say we must come back tomorrow, but today, if we will hear Your voice, You will hear us.

You brought light out of darkness, not out of lesser light. You can bring Thy summer out of winter, though You have no spring. All occassions invite Your mercies and all times are Your seasons.

John Donne

Comfort

Remember the Lord

In my distress I called to the LORD, and he answered me. From the depths of the grave I called for help, and you listened to my cry.

You hurled me into the deep, into the very heart of the seas, and the currents swirled about me ...

I said, 'I have been banished from your sight; yet I will look again toward your holy temple.'

But you brought my life up from the pit, O LORD my God.

When my life was ebbing away, I remembered you, LORD, and my prayer rose to you, to your holy temple.

Those who cling to worthless idols forfeit the grace that could be theirs.

But I, with a song of thanksgiving, will sacrifice to you. What I have vowed I will make good. Salvation comes from the LORD.

Jonah 2:2-4, 6-9

Jonah

A child's bedtime prayer

Now I lay me down to sleep,
   I pray Thee, Lord,
   Thy child to keep;
   Thy love go with me
   all the night
   and wake me
   with the morning light.

Now I lay me down to sleep,
   I pray Thee, Lord,
   my soul to keep;
   and should I die
   before I wake,
   I trust, Thee, Lord,
   my soul to take.

Traditional

Comfort

Mourning into dancing

I will exalt you, O LORD, for you lifted me out of the depths. O LORD my God, I called to you for help and you healed me.

O LORD, you brought me up from the grave; you spared me from going down into the pit.

O LORD, when you favored me, you made my mountain stand firm; but when you hid your face, I was dismayed.

To you, O LORD, I called; to the Lord I cried for mercy: "What gain is there in my destruction, in my going down into the pit? Hear, O LORD, and be merciful to me; O LORD, be my help."

You turned my wailing into dancing; you removed my sackcloth and clothed me with joy, that my heart may sing to you and not be silent. O LORD my God, I will give you thanks forever.

Psalm 30:1-3, 7-12

David

When God seems far away

How long, O LORD? Will you forget me forever?
How long will you hide your face from me?
How long must I wrestle with my thoughts
    and every day have sorrow in my heart?
How long will my enemy triumph over me?
Look on me and answer, O LORD my God.
Give light to my eyes, or I will sleep in death;
    my enemy will say, "I have overcome him,"
    and my foes will rejoice when I fall.
But I trust in your unfailing love;
    my heart rejoices in your salvation.
I will sing to the LORD,
    for he has been good to me.

Psalm 13

David

Comfort

Rest for the weary

I praise you, Father,
    Lord of heaven and earth,
    because you have hidden these things
    from the wise and learned,
    and revealed them to little children.
    Yes, Father, for this was your good pleasure.
Come to me,
    all you who are weary and burdened,
    and I will give you rest.
Take my yoke upon you and learn from me,
    for I am gentle and humble in heart,
    and you will find rest for your souls.
For my yoke is easy and my burden is light.

Matthew 11:25-26, 28-30

Jesus

In wrath remember mercy

LORD, I have heard of your fame; I stand in awe of your deeds, O LORD. Renew them in our day, in our time make them known; in wrath remember mercy.

Were you angry with the rivers, O LORD? Was your wrath against the streams? Did you rage against the sea when you rode with your horses and your victorious chariots?

You split the earth with rivers; the mountains saw you and writhed. Torrents of water swept by; the deep roared and lifted its waves on high.

In wrath you strode through the earth and in anger you threshed the nations.

You came out to deliver your people, to save your anointed one.

Habakkuk 3:2, 8-10, 12-13

Habakkuk

Comfort

Protection in the day of despair

Heal me, O LORD, and I will be healed; save me and I will be saved, for you are the one I praise.

They keep saying to me, "Where is the word of the LORD? Let it now be fulfilled!"

I have not run away from being your shepherd; you know I have not desired the day of despair. What passes my lips is open before you.

Do not be a terror to me; you are my refuge in the day of disaster.

Let my persecutors be put to shame, but keep me from shame; let them be terrified, but keep me from terror. Bring on them the day of disaster; destroy them with double destruction.

Jeremiah 17:14-18

Jeremiah

Restoration

Praise our God, O peoples, let the sound of his praise be heard; he has preserved our lives and kept our feet from slipping.

For you, O God, tested us; you refined us like silver.

You brought us into prison and laid burdens on our backs.

You let men ride over our heads; we went through fire and water, but you brought us to a place of abundance.

I will come to your temple with burnt offerings and fulfill my vows to you – vows my lips promised and my mouth spoke when I was in trouble.

I will sacrifice fat animals to you and an offering of rams; I will offer bulls and goats. *Selah*

Psalm 66:8-15

Unknown

The Apostles' creed

I believe in God, the Father Almighty, maker of heaven and earth: and in Jesus Christ His Only Son Our Lord, who was conceived by the Holy Spirit, born of the Virgin Mary, suffered under Pontius Pilate, was crucified, died and was buried.

He descended into hell; the third day He rose again from the dead. He ascended into heaven, and sitteth at the right hand of God the Father Almighty; from thence He shall come to judge the living and the dead.

I believe in the Holy Spirit; the holy Christian church; the communion of saints; the forgiveness of sins; the resurrection of the body, and life everlasting.

Amen.

Traditional